D1269035

Folk Kilns I

FAMOUS CERAMICS OF JAPAN 3

Folk Kilns I

Hiroshi Mizuo

KODANSHA INTERNATIONAL LTD.
Tokyo, New York, San Francisco

distributed in the United States by Kodansha International/USA, Ltd.,
through Harper & Row, Publishers, Inc., 10 East 53rd Street,
New York, New York 10022

published by Kodansha International Ltd., 12–21 Otowa 2-chome,
Bunkyo-ku, Tokyo 112 and Kodansha International/USA, Ltd., 10 East
53rd Street, New York, New York 10022 and 44 Montgomery Street,
San Francisco, California 94104

copyright © 1981 by Kodansha International Ltd.
all rights reserved
printed in Japan
first edition, 1981

LCC 80–84463
ISBN 0–87011–416–6
JBC 1072–789457–2361

Folk Kilns of Honshu

The two volumes on folk kilns in this *Famous Ceramics of Japan* series introduce kilns from throughout the Japanese archipelago that produced general utility ceramics in the past, those that have continued to the present as part of this stream, and those that have been newly established. Honshu folk kilns are gathered in volume I, while volume II tours kiln sites on the three other main areas of the Japanese archipelago—Shikoku, Kyushu, and Okinawa.

It is impossible within this limited number of pages to exhaustively introduce the extensive range of good ceramics produced at the large number of folk kilns, thus I have confined myself to the principal kilns and their products, of which I have selected only a very few. However, because of this very abundance of beautiful pots, as great a number of choice examples as space permits are collected here.

Folk objects differ from articles produced for the upper classes, especially exclusive goods produced at government kilns (note 1) and fief kilns (note 2); from tea ceremony wares, which show a contrived rusticity; and from works by individual artist-potters, whose object has always been to express their own subjective sense of beauty. The practicality of folk wares; their cheap production in large numbers; their production by artisans not possessing particularly outstanding talents; their traditional character, which is based on accumulated experience; their naturalness; and their use of local materials and specialties, all are qualities that have molded their personality and define their charm. If one was to describe the beauty of folk ceramics in a nutshell, likewise the beauty of all proper folkcrafts, the most suitable expression would probably be "healthy beauty."

Selecting tea ceremony utensils from the general utility vessels of China, Korea, various South Sea Islands, and also from the folk kilns of Japan, the early tea masters termed this healthiness *wabi*. *Wabi* is the aesthetic concept around which the tea ceremony developed; it emphasizes simplicity, humility, and intense appreciation of the immediate experience. Since about 1925, thanks to Muneyoshi Yanagi (note 3) and his followers, the beauty of folk kilns has become widely recognized. Interest also turned to the general utility ceramics of such kilns as Seto, Shigaraki, Bizen, Kutani, and Imari, which thus far were renowned mainly for their production of fine porcelains and tea wares.

Proper folk kiln ceramics are those that fulfill the basic nature of craft—that is, to satisfy both beauty and utility—and could well be called the mainstream of all pottery and porcelain. The charm one feels when one looks at folkcraft articles, when one touches them, and when one uses them, arises from precisely the beauty of utility.

Tōhoku District (Aomori, Akita, Iwate, Miyagi, Yamagata, and Fukushima prefectures)

Generally speaking, the northern provinces, where the winter is harsh and the snowfall heavy, do not provide a suitable climate for ceramics. However, since utensils used in daily life had to be produced, not a few folk kilns were active in the Tōhoku (northeastern) region. The bulk of them were the "courtyard" kilns (note 4) of feudal lords or fief kilns, which served as the foundation for the later development of folk kilns, but there were also pure folk kilns. Just as in the other districts, in Tōhoku kilns also began to be established after the beginning of the Edo period (mid seventeenth century), but the nineteenth century (late Edo period and the Meiji period) can be considered their zenith. Kilns were first established in Miyagi and Fukushima prefectures in the south of the Tōhoku region, then ceramic production spread north into Yamagata, Akita, Iwate, and Aomori prefectures.

Aizu-Hongō and Sōma in Fukushima Prefecture

and Kirigome and Tsutsumi in Miyagi Prefecture were the first kilns of the Tōhoku area. All were founded in the latter half of the seventeenth century as fief kilns.

Aizu-Hongō ware production, building on the techniques of unglazed tile manufacture, started on the foundation of the fief kiln established by Mizuno Genzaemon, who was called from Seto in Shōhō 2 (1645). At the beginning of the eighteenth century, it was converted into a folk kiln, and the production quantity was also increased; then, sometime just before the nineteenth century, it began to fire porcelain wares. Until the beginning of the Meiji period, some ten kilns in the area were making pottery, while the remainder produced porcelains. Gradually this number of pottery-firing kilns diminished, until in the Shōwa period (1926-present) the Munakata kiln alone fired stoneware.

The Munakata kiln, motivated by the folkcraft movement, has continued its trade to the present, retaining the quality of a genuine folk kiln. It makes general utility wares with white, green, *ame* (amber; note 7), and *namako* (note 8) glazes on strong forms.

Sōma ware includes Sōma-Koma ware made at an official kiln said to have been founded in Kan'ei 7 (1630) by Tashiro Gengoemon, who had studied in Kyoto, and the ware of the Ōhori kiln, which opened in the early years of the eighteenth century under the fief's patronage.

The latter was a folk kiln. When it thrived, from the early to mid nineteenth century, thirty-five kilns were run by one hundred potter households. They continued their work even after the Meiji period (1868–1912), and at present there are some twenty households carrying on the trade, but compared to the distinctive products of the past, such as saké bottles and pouring bowls, the wares today have declined. This phenomenon is not unique to this area.

Within the same Sōma area, a kiln called Tatenoshita in Nakamura is presumed to have been founded in the early eighteenth century, and a great variety of utility ware fired there from the latter years of the Edo period to the early years of the Shōwa period (1926–present) have been excavated in recent years. Using ceramic processes very similar to those of Tsutsumi ware (discussed below), various types of large storage jars were the principal product. It is said that retainers of Okada Kenmotsu, minister to the daimyo of Sōma fief, produced general utility wares for the common

people as a secondary occupation. These are vigorous, lively folk wares.

Kirigome ware in Miyagi Prefecture is an underglaze cobalt decorated porcelain ware, and among such pieces as barrel-shaped saké bottles, a few distinctive old works remain. The date of the kiln's opening and the particulars of its transformation from an official kiln to a folk kiln are unknown, thus an investigation of the kiln ruins north of Sendai would be welcomed. The first porcelain production in the northeast region is assumed to have been at Aizu-Hongō, but the roots of Kirigome ware may trace back even further.

Representing Tsutsumi ware, also in Miyagi Prefecture, only the solitary Hariu kiln presently remains, but from the end of the Edo period through the beginning of the Meiji period, this was a folk kiln region brimming with activity. Tiles had been made from ancient times in the vicinity of the town of Tsutsumi northeast of Sendai City; then it became a production center in the medieval period (and in recent times) for a variety of unglazed earthenware. At the beginning of the seventeenth century, with the Daté clan's establishment of a castle in Sendai and the accompanying build-up of the castle town, Tsutsumi resurrected its ceramic industry by producing black roof tiles. Subsequently, Uemura Man'emon was ordered by the fief in Genroku 7 (1694), to improve and make this ceramic industry self-supporting, and he operated an official kiln making Sugiyama ware. That became a folk kiln and continued to produce everyday kitchen utensils for the fief's populace. Despite ups and downs, Tsutsumi prospered as a pottery town until the Meiji Restoration (1868), making large vessels such as storage vats and jars and mass-producing diverse utility vessels. Large storage jars with a rice-bran-ash white glaze (note 6) dramatically imposed on a black glaze (note 5) ground, together with the Tatenoshita wares, are outstanding examples of northeastern folk ceramics. It appears that the name "Tsutsumi ware" came into use roughly after 1897.

In Yamagata Prefecture ceramics are being produced presently only at Hirashimizu and Shinjō, but previously there were folk kilns at Narushima and Kaminohata, established at the end of the eighteenth century, and Daihōji, established at the beginning of the nineteenth century. In Narushima ware of Yonezawa, the technical influence of Aizu-Hongō ware is discernible. This kiln came under the fief's patronage, as did several other similar kilns.

Hirashimizu ware was founded at the beginning of the nineteenth century on the southeast foot of Chitose Mountain in Yamagata Prefecture, producing stoneware in the Sōma-Kasama ware vein and porcelain in the Imari tradition. Its utility vessels, locally called *tsuchi-yaki* (literally, "earthenware") are especially good. There was an ample variety of unpatterned white slip-coated pieces, *ame* glaze (note 7), black glaze (note 5), and applied decoration. It continues to operate today but is apparently groping to find direction as a contemporary folk kiln.

Shinjō ware (Higashiyama ware) is located on the outskirts of Shinjō City, and it is said to have been founded in Tempō 12 (1841). The glaze application, using *namako* glaze (note 8), is lively, and its three-legged cooking pots were outstanding examples of Japanese kitchenware. Daihōji kiln ruins were excavated in Daihōji and Shinmachi within Tsuruoka City. This presumably was a successful folk kiln in the first half of the nineteenth century. Its technology is of the same derivation as Shinjō ware, and its products are similar.

In Akita Prefecture, Shiraiwa ware, begun around Meiwa 7 (1770) by a potter from Sōma named Matsumoto Unshichi, is the oldest. This folk kiln continued until approximately Meiji 30 (1897) and was characterized by *namako* glaze (note 8) applied over a brown base glaze on the inside and part or all of the outside of vessels.

In Senpoku County there was a small utility vessel kiln called Kurisawa, but in approximately Shōwa 10 (1935) production was terminated. Also in Senpoku County, Naraoka ware has persisted to the present day, having been founded by Komatsu Seiji in Bunkyu 3 (1863), after he left the Shiraiwa kiln. It was a genuine local kiln in its prime during the Meiji period. Powerful, sturdy storage jars, food bowls, and pouring bowls were produced by this kiln.

In Iwate Prefecture, Kuji ware is produced in Kuji City. In Bunsei 5 (1822), at the instigation of Kumagai Jin'emon, who was trained at Sōma, it was converted from an official clan kiln to a folk kiln. The subdued old works, with *ame* glaze (note 7) applied over a dark brown background, are stolid, and the pouring bowls, with a white glaze and compressed forms, are especially new and refreshing. Ceramic

cups for the sauce in which *soba* (buckwheat noodles) are dipped, rare in the northeast, were made. Their descendants are called Kokuji ware ("little" Kuji ware, not "old" Kuji ware) and continue to be produced today. Also in Iwate Prefecture there was Nagashima ware. Its roots are thought to lie in Shiraiwa ware.

In Aomori Prefecture on Honshu's northern shore, Akudo ware, founded in the beginning of the nineteenth century, was in operation until the Taishō years (1912–25). Saké bottles, fire containers, and cylinders for hot water were produced for local use only and were distinguished by tube-trailed decoration. At present, there are several up-and-coming small folk kilns in this prefecture.

Kantō District (Ibaragi, Tochigi, Gunma, Saitama, Kanagawa, and Chiba prefectures, and metropolitan Tokyo) and Kōshinetsu District (Yamanashi, Nagano, and Niigata prefectures)

The Kantō district contained urban Edo (present-day Tokyo), a major consumer area with demand for great quantities of utility wares. Aside from what the large production centers supplied in response to that demand, there were also utility ware kilns within the city of Edo; and while it is conceivable that folk kilns were operated in each of the various Kantō provinces, the known folk kilns are limited to Kasama in Ibaragi Prefecture and Mashiko and Koisago in Tochigi Prefecture.

Production of Kasama ware was initiated in the An'ei years (1772–81), first as a "courtyard" ceramic (note 4) of the feudal lord Makino by a potter engaged from Shigaraki; then, commencing in the Ka'ei years (1848–54), daily use pots for the neighboring farming population began to be produced. The Shishido kiln, of Sōma extraction, was nearby, and the two kilns developed while mutually influencing each other.

Ōtsuka Keizaburō established Mashiko ware production in Ka'ei 6 (1853) in conjunction with Kasama potters. Because the Kurowa fief lord, Ōzeki, granted his patronage with a view to promoting fief industry, it gradually came to thrive as the largest ceramics industry center in the Kantō area. It also had the benefit of proximity to Edo, and responded to the demand there for kitchen utensils. In the process, techniques from Kasama, Sōma, Aizu, Shigaraki, and Kyoto were introduced, and the raw materials and techniques for applied decoration on white slip-coated wares were developed. A sturdy constitution and the taut dignity representative of the Kantō region can be seen as the focus of old Mashiko products. The techniques for making teapots with landscape or plum motifs were garnered from Shigaraki and Kasama and cultivated as a special production item of Mashiko ware. After Shōji Hamada (note 9) settled in this town, Mashiko ware became widely known to the world and is perhaps the pottery town presently exhibiting the most vigor.

Koisago ware also belongs to the Kasama lineage and began production in approximately the middle of the nineteenth century near Karasuyama. In addition, the Magashima kiln in Tochigi Prefecture was a local kiln for earthenware, which after the war made newly designed red and black braziers, planters, stools, flower containers, and brush holders, but is no longer in operation.

The vestiges of Hannō ware in Saitama Prefecture indicate that it enjoyed considerable success as a local kiln.

In the adjacent Kōshinetsu district, Nōana ware in Yamanashi Prefecture, Ōbayashi and Tenryūkyō wares in Nagano Prefecture, and Anchi and Sado wares in Niigata Prefecture are in operation at present. However, outstanding pieces are scarce. Compared to those, the old ceramics produced at one time by folk kilns throughout present Nagano Prefecture are quite satisfying. Matsushiro ware in the vicinity of Matsushiro, Suzaka ware in Suzaka, Uematsu ware in Nagano, Okada ware in Yashiro, Someya and Tōma wares in Ueda, Irisawa and Maeyama wares in Saku, Sōdōji ware in Ikeda, Seba ware in Seba, Akabane ware in Tatsuno, Takatō ware in Takatō, and Kazakoshi, Imada, Ogawa, Kitsuzan, and Obayashi wares in Iida are all worthy of note. Selected representative pieces of some of these kilns are illustrated in this volume.

Matsushiro ware is a general term for a host of fief kilns and folk kilns in the vicinity of Matsushiro, which waxed and waned from Bunka 13 (1816), when the Matsushiro fief opened the Terao Myōun and Tennō Zan kilns, to the beginning of the Shōwa period. Primarily everyday utility vessels, including varieties of large and small storage vats and jars,

large utility bowls, food bowls, plates, saké bottles and cups, cooking pots, braziers, etc. were fired. The volume of production is conjectured to have been enormous throughout that period. Just as at other folk kilns, production at the Matsushiro kilns was sufficient to supply the majority of the utility wares needed by the people of the province until the kilns were driven out of business by the goods of the large mass-production centers with the opening of the railroads. The clay was coarse, heavy, and strong, and mixed hardwood-ash glazes, feldspathic glazes, straw-ash glazes, *ame* glazes (note 7), and copper glazes were used, frequently ornamented with an additional application of green glaze.

Nyūdō ware was begun in Ansei 6 (1859) by Tanaka Gozaemon as a fief kiln, then converted to a folk kiln in the Meiji period, existing until 1918. Water storage jars, mortars, teapots, saké bottles, and oil lamp dishes, etc., as well as pots called "fishermen's helmets" for catching shrimp in Suwa Lake, were all produced. Because Gozaemon's younger brother, Shigeta, went to Seba to manage the Yamazaki kiln, the technical relationship between the two kilns is presumed to have been close.

Seba ware includes the products of the Yamazaki and Kamijo kilns, both of which rose during the latter days of the Edo period and had died out by the end of the Meiji period. In the Seto manner, *namako* glaze (note 8) applied over brown or black was prevalent, and, again, water storage vats, "helmet" bowls (note 10), saké bottles, etc., were produced. The second decade of the Meiji period appears to have been Seba's most successful, when master artisans such as Okuda Shinsai were active, and records show that ware was made not only for the home province but was distributed throughout the entire Kōshinetsu and Kantō regions.

Someya ware is an unglazed ceramic ware fired to vitrification. The date of the kiln's founding is unknown. It appears to have been at its most prosperous around the Tenmei era (1781–89) and closed around 1933. The powerful forms created by firing the clay to vitrification without a glaze, a technique in use since ancient times, and the color tones produced by accidental ash glaze effects combine to produce a healthy, austere beauty. Pre-Meiji Someya ware, which was fired in rifle kilns (note 11), is especially worthy of attention.

Takatō ware was initiated at the mandate of the

fief by a potter from Mino, Uhyōe, in Bunka 10 (1813). In Tempō 12 (1841), production was transferred to private management, and the number of kilns increased slightly, with the last, the Marusen kiln, persisting until about 1960. All kinds of pots were mass-produced, and many remain today. Use of white *namako* glaze (note 8) is a specialty.

The products of these diverse kilns are still used today as utility vessels by households throughout this area. It is a wonder that Nagano Prefecture, which was once suitable country for folk kilns, today does not possess a noteworthy ceramic industry.

Chūbu District (Shizuoka, Aichi, and Gifu prefectures)

In Aichi and Gifu prefectures, which had supported large ceramic industry centers such as Seto, Tokoname, and Mino since ancient times, a large number of folk kilns contended with each other from the beginning. The diversity that allowed elite wares, common wares, and also tea ceremony ceramics to be fired at the same kilns here, as in the northern Kyushu area, is most surprising. However, old Seto ware, old Tokoname ware, and the Mino tea ceramics will be entrusted to other volumes, and attention will be given the utility ware kilns that flourished in the nineteenth century.

Within the diverse wares produced at Seto, which has endured since ancient times as one of Japan's major ceramic production centers, the utility wares of its folk kilns radiated a brilliance not evident at other provincial kilns and brought color to the lives of the common people of the eighteenth and nineteenth centuries. This brilliance is one of warmth and intimacy, not the beauty of extravagance. One representative Seto product is the so-called stone plates (*ishi-zara*; also known by other names), familiar to travelers at the inns of the station towns and roadside teahouses up and down the fifty-three stations of the Tōkaidō (the travel route extending from Edo to Kyoto) and also found on the dining table of every household. Kilns in Seto extended from Seto-no-Hora to all of Kita-Shindani. The stone plates were made in large and small sizes, the forms are thick, and indigo and dark brown designs were applied using local natural cobalt (note 12) and iron oxide (note 13). The color tones are modest, but the adroit

brushes of the decorators painted landscapes, flowers and birds, and men and beasts, all livelier than the real objects. These artisans, who decorated wares quickly, in large quantities, and cheaply, with a minimum of effort, have left behind paintings rivaling even those of master artists.

The famous "horse-eye plates" (*uma no me zara*), which perform the same function as stone plates, were produced in the vicinity of Seto-no-Hora.

Oil plates (*abura-zara*; so-called because they were placed under oil-burning lanterns to catch oil), also called *andon* plates (an *andon* is a paper-covered, oil-burning lamp), appear at approximately the beginning of the nineteenth century to replace the previously metal *andon* oil plates. They were used until the Meiji period, when kerosene lamps made their appearance. Primarily fired at the Shinano and Akazu kilns in Seto, they were able to be made in large numbers when kiln technology overcame the difficulties of keeping plates from warping when firing them in stacks. At first, chrysanthemum designs were scattered on a green Oribe glaze, but before long, a variety of pictorial designs were also applied in iron pigment. Representing what must be termed the height of skill, these refreshing designs must have offered bright diversion to the people of the Edo period living with the dim *andon* lighting. Along with the stone plates, horse-eye plates and oil plates were also made in large quantities.

The Seto folk kilns made and fired anything, including food bowls with grass and flowers, pines, bamboos, and willows applied by a mature brush; tableware with thin red, brown, and indigo vertical stripes, known as the "wheat-straw" pattern; various saké bottles displaying the pattern of rough brush-strokes alone; various storage jars with the *ame* glaze (note 7); white storage jars and rouge pots (note 14); water storage jars; pouring bowls; various mortars; incense burners, either green-glazed or cobalt under-glaze decorated; water droppers—all show highly developed decorative techniques. Such decorated ware is known as *e-Seto* ("picture" Seto). Shino and Oribe wares started in this area in the Momoyama period (1573–1615), and these styles continue today. Along with the porcelains of Imari in the west and Kutani in the north, the colorful world of Japanese ceramic decoration is seen here.

In the nineteenth century, though in Seto the majority of folk kilns were converted into porcelain kilns, stoneware preserved a healthy tradition. One such kiln operates in Seto-no-Hora and continues to produce lovely, contemporary utility wares. The dignified two- and three-colored "lotus" bowls depicted on the cover of this volume are newly designed products of this Mizuno kiln. Contemporary *e-Seto* tableware is also created here.

In contrast to Seto's comparatively urban orientation, focusing on the production of small utility wares, Tokoname fired large objects, beginning in the twelfth and thirteenth centuries, to meet the needs of farming villages. These are water storage jars, cinerary urns, grain storage jars, large bowls, and a variety of large plates. In the late Edo period, Shudei ware (note 15) production started. In present-day Tokoname, it is regrettable that there are only mechanically manufactured industrial ceramics such as drainage pipes and tiles and the works of artist-potters, but no authentic folk kilns. This is also common in Mino. Neighboring Seto, Mino has enjoyed an intimate interchange with Seto since ancient times. The potters of Seto together with the craftsmen of Mino performed a major role in the creation of tea ceramics, namely, Yellow Seto *(ki-Zeto)*, Black Seto *(Seto-guro)*, Shino, and Oribe, which flowered from the sixteenth century until about 1630.

The conventional view of craft history claims that Mino ware declined during the Edo period, when tea ceramics were supplanted by general, everyday utility wares. This biased view of ceramic history places greatest value on the elegant wares, and ignores the wholesome beauty of utility wares made at folk kilns. Mino tea ceramics did decline, but that richness of skill and experience was preserved in the world of folk kilns, and superb utility wares continued to be made. Indeed, it must be said that among the utility wares of Mino, which discarded and left behind the conscious artificiality of the tea ceremony and recaptured the beauty arising from function, there are some pieces worthy of being used as tea vessels, in the original spirit and meaning of the tea aesthetic.

From the middle through the late Edo period, undecorated wares were fired at various kilns, glazed with yellow Seto *(ki-Zeto)* or iron glazes. These can be widely seen on a variety of storage jars, large bowls, plates, food bowls, and saké bottles. It is thought that large quantities of water droppers were mold-formed at some Mino kilns.

Upon entering the Meiji period, Mino became an industrial ceramic manufacturing area. Its brilliant history and achievements are today being wiped out by a jumble of factory products and the works of artist-potters.

One additional Gifu Prefecture ware is Shibukusa ware of Takayama in Hida. Koito ware and Yamada ware also exist in Takayama, but Shibukusa ware, including both stoneware and porcelain, is the most famous. The personality of contemporary Shibukusa ware, as a special product of Takayama, is becoming stronger. However, at one time it must have been a folk kiln that circulated its products widely throughout the area encompassing parts of Gifu, Niigata, Fukui, and Toyama prefectures. The simple motifs of the old underglaze cobalt decorated porcelains are rather good. Even among today's works, if one is selective, fresh designs can be found.

Hokuriku District (Toyama, Fukui, and Ishikawa prefectures)

The Hokuriku district is also a vigorous center of ceramics. Toyama Prefecture received Seto's influence; Fukui Prefecture has its ancient Echizen ware; and Ishikawa Prefecture has the colorful Kutani ware tradition, with its intimate relationship with the Imari polychrome porcelains. The special features of these great traditions are also reflected in the folk kilns.

The oldest ceramic kiln of Toyama Prefecture is Etchū-Seto in the town of Tateyama, which opened in Bunraku 2 (1593). The lord Maeda Toshinaga called a potter named Hikoemon from Owari and, along with having him make tea wares, had him fire utility vessels for the fief's domestic use. Subsequently, Seto potters were repeatedly called upon to transmit new techniques. In the late seventeenth century, twenty kilns were active, and until the Meiji period this was the major production center of the area. From the end of the Meiji through the Taishō period, it was temporarily discontinued, but was again revived in the Shōwa period and is active today. Since potters of this kiln were trained at Seto, their work is sound and techniques similar.

The "duck" saké bottles (the name may come from the fact that the pond where the clay was mined was famous for ducks) and *bote-bote* teabowls (note 16) made here are replete with local flavor.

Next there is Kosugi ware in the town of Kosugi, said to have been established at the end of the sixteenth century. This kiln, too, was active as a folk kiln at the end of the Edo period, and while concentrating on the production of celadon, made a great range of other types, including *ame* and white-glazed, stylish tea wares, liquor vessels, tablewares, calligraphy accessories, and religious vessels. Although essentially a folk kiln, its products satisfied urban tastes. In addition to Kosugi, some twenty other minor folk kilns in Toyama Prefecture have appeared and disappeared since the end of the Edo period.

Fukui Prefecture is the home of Echizen ware. Tracing its history back to the end of the Heian period (twelfth century), it made the transition from Sue ware (high-fired, dark-gray thin stoneware with a hard, fine texture made from approximately A.D. 400 to 1200) to stoneware high-fired to vitrification, and developed as a sibling of old Tokoname ware. The Echizen kilns, which began by making cinerary urns along with everyday utensils, entered a stage of firing robust, oversized storage vats, storage jars, and tubs, then developed into a folk kiln producing Oda ware. Utility vessels such as water storage, grain storage, and pickle storage jars were produced for the rural population. Although the forms were austere and unpretentious, lively drip-glazes were sometimes applied. At present a ceramic-arts community is operating as part of a project for the renaissance of Echizen ware, but a revival of the brawny attraction of the old works is to be desired.

A local kiln called Hisaka flourished in Takefu in the Meiji period. Utility wares mainly employing *tenmoku* glaze (note 17) were fired here, and although its storage vats and storage jars exhibited rather creditable techniques, in recent years they suddenly lost their strength.

Kutani ware of Ishikawa Prefecture and the wares of Imari (Arita) are the most famous of Japan's enamel-decorated porcelains. A recent theory concerning Kutani's origin suggests that the ware was first produced in the Imari area, further intensifying the controversy surrounding these porcelains. Undoubtedly there are Imari pieces among the wares known as old Kutani, but there is no doubt that Kutani pieces reflecting the richness of Kaga Province (the present-day greater Kanazawa area) were created where Kutani is still made today. Old Kutani

pieces with simple overglaze enamel decoration can be regarded as embodying the personality of folk wares, though Kutani was established purely as a fief kiln. After the Edo period, Kutani ware became almost entirely privately managed. Because of the brilliance of these enameled porcelains, one may question putting them in the same category as most of the other folk kiln products reproduced here. However, this ware is one manifestation of the beauty of crafts serving the lives of an urban population.

Kinki District (metropolitan Osaka and Kyoto, and Nara, Wakayama, Mie, and Hyōgo prefectures)

The Kinki district, long-time the heartland of Japan, preserves the history of the evolution of ceramics in capsul form. Metropolitan Osaka embraces Japan's oldest Sue ware village. Government kilns were operated in Nara Prefecture. Shigaraki, one of what have come to be called the "Six Ancient Kilns," was located in Shiga Prefecture. Tamba, also one of the so-called Six Ancient Kilns, should be included within this sphere of influence.

Iga ware, a tea ceramic, was made in Mie Prefecture. Also in Mie Prefecture, ceramics ranging from Banko enamel-decorated wares to the contemporary ceramics and porcelain industries of Kuwana and Yokkaichi can be found. In Kyoto, the very urban Kyoto ware prospered, while sundry tea ceramics and individual artist-potters rose and fell. Let us single out from among these the most important folk ceramics made from the middle Edo period on.

In the diverse ceramic and porcelain vessels included in Kyoto ware, the utility vessels used by the common people of Kyoto must naturally be considered. However, the tastes of urban life called for excessive refinement of and ornamentation on utility pots, and the tendency to obscure any truly healthy, utilitarian beauty was strong. It can be assumed that the pots used in Kyoto kitchens came from provincial production centers. Desirable Kyoto ware utility vessels in recent times have been made at the Kawai kiln (note 18) after the rise of the folkcraft movement.

As the tea ceremony flourished, the bond between Shigaraki ware in Shiga Prefecture and the tea masters was deeply forged, and Shigaraki became known as a tea ceramics kiln. At the same time, the production of folk ceramics was also vigorous, and from the middle Edo period on, Shigaraki was a large production center. The list of storage jars alone is diverse, comprising those made for *umeboshi* (pickled plums), water, *miso* (fermented bean paste), oil, confections, tooth blackening materials, and leaf tea, while the production of saké bottles, storage bottles, braziers, diverse cooking pots, mortars, teapots, plates, and sundry food bowls swelled to enormous quantities. Those pots were conveyed by boat down the Kizu and Yodo rivers, forwarded to Kyoto, Osaka, and Sakai, then distributed to western Japan. Tea-leaf storage jars were the most famous, being made exclusively at a kiln in the Nagano area and marketed through the Uji teahouses. Jars with a green glaze poured over a white ground are typical, and a considerable number remain today. Furthermore, the Koyama kiln specialized principally in the production of teapots. Teapots with landscape designs were popular, and this style was passed on to kilns in Akashi, Kasama, and Mashiko in the north and to Noma in Kyushu in the south. Regrettably, contemporary Shigaraki seems to be destroying its own heritage and tradition.

In Mie Prefecture there is Iga ware. Sharing the same technical background as Shigaraki, it is renowned for its tea ceramics, but it originally fired utility wares for farm households as a local kiln. Marubashira kiln is the center of folk kiln Iga ware. It fired various cooking pots, teapots, and diverse tableware, and has been active from the Tempō era (1830–44). The teapots competed well with those of Shigaraki and became popular. The ample forms of the so-called green teapots and the ingenuity of their lovely green glaze are prominent features. In the mid 1920s, the beloved *kisha dobin*, the little teapots holding a small amount of hot tea sold on station platforms throughout the country, were made in quantity.

Yokkaichi City, also in Mie Prefecture, is famous for Banko ware, established during the Gembun era (1736–41) by a wealthy merchant of Kuwana, Nunami Rōzan. Banko ware production has spread to many places, but pieces that can be considered folk ceramics are rare. The enameled incense stands in Plate 3 are examples of fine Banko pieces.

Akahada ware is found in Nara Prefecture, and as well as being counted among the Seven Enshū

Kilns (note 19), it also fired everyday utility vessels. These are still being fired today. Among the articles produced near the end of the Edo period, some pleasant ones may be found.

Situated in modern Hyōgo Prefecture are the Tamba kilns. Tamba ware began in the Kamakura period (1185–1333) and has continued to the present, and although Kobori Enshū ordered the production of tea wares there, Tamba never sacrificed its folk-kiln honesty. The beauty of old Tamba deserves an entire book; here a look at Tamba ware after kilns were organized in the village of Tachikui in Hōreki 2 (1752) will suffice. Tamba of the middle period had gone from the thick, vitrified ware with natural ash-glaze effects (old Tamba ware) to the use of red-brown and black glazes in the early Edo period. Thereafter, new styles developed, including use of white slip as an engobe and for tube-trailed decoration, "ink flow" effects (note 21), and some enamel decoration, while Tamba's repertoire of products expanded from large forms such as storage vats, storage jars, and "boat" saké bottles (so-called because a wide, flat base kept them stable when a boat rolled and pitched), to a great range and variety of utility pots. This florescence resulted from the prosperity of urban Osaka and Kyoto. The beautiful natural ash-glaze effects (note 22), Tamba's greatest charm, disappeared, but, on the other hand, a unique elegance, harmonizing rusticity and refinement, was born. Simple, distinctive techniques of decoration such as drip glazing, incising, and impressed leaves were perfected. This tradition is still maintained today, and Tachikui pottery continues as a contemporary folk ware, one of the few such direct descendants of the past.

San'in District (Tottori and Shimane prefectures)

The area of modern Tottori and Shimane prefectures is also one of ceramic activity, where a large number of folk kilns have appeared and disappeared since about the middle of the eighteenth century. In the early Shōwa period (after 1925), the region was quick to promote the new folkcraft movement along with its native handwork.

Included in the folk kilns of Tottori Prefecture are Aimi ware, Hōshōji ware, Ochiai ware, Karo ware,

Tokunage ware, Fukui ware, Hamasaka ware, Utsuro ware, Yoshinari ware, Uradome ware, Maruyama ware, Higeta ware, and Ushinoto ware; these include both pottery and porcelain used in this area as everyday pots. The fact that porcelain wares, continuing the Imari underglaze cobalt decorative techniques, were fired at Utsuro, Yoshinari, Uradome, and Maruyama kilns is noteworthy. Among the utility porcelain wares today attributed to Imari kilns, a considerable number are thought to have actually been fired at kilns in the San'in area, as well as in Tōhoku and Shikoku. Although only one underglaze cobalt decorated lidded storage jar from Yoshinari kiln is included here (Plate 6), many extant pieces are known.

Among the many that abandoned production, the Ushinoto kiln alone was revived in the late 1920s as a contemporary folk kiln through the endeavors of Shōya Yoshida (note 23), a leader of the San'in New Folkcraft Movement, and has persisted to the present time. A potter from Iwami opened this kiln in the Tempō era (1830–44); then from the end of the Edo period through the Meiji years, a variety of saké bottles, "Gorohachi" teabowls, pickle plates, storage jars, and food bowls was fired, then covered with transparent, black, or green glazes and decorated in iron or white slip. These goods spread beyond the original area to adjacent districts, while "vinegar bottles" were transported in large quantities as far as Hokkaido. Subsequent to its revival, this kiln has been turning out new designs of contemporary tableware. The Nakai kiln, in the vicinity of the Ushinoto kiln, and the Uradome kiln are two more folk kilns revived under Shōya Yoshida's leadership.

The ceramics of two contrasting areas of Shimane Prefecture—tranquil, delicate Izumo and strong, harsh Iwami—reflect the temperaments of their places of manufacture.

Kinzan ware, Komondō ware, Sarayama ware, Mori ware, and Hachiman ware were all established in the vicinity of Yasuki City, and with the exception of Sarayama, are thriving today. The Mori kiln is one of the few local kilns that has managed to maintain the character of a traditional folk kiln. Several folk kilns also flourished around Lake Shinji. Usually referred to by the general term Fujina ware, the Yumachi, Hōonji, Fujina, and Sodeshi kilns are included. All are functioning as contemporary folk kilns, except for Hōonji.

The Yumachi kiln was founded in 1923 and began making new, contemporary tablewares on the occasion of a visit by Sōetsu Yanagi (the founder of the folkcraft movement) to San'in. As with Fujina ware, its specialty is the production of Western-style tableware with a galena glaze (note 24).

The Sodeshi kiln opened in 1894 and also later participated in the folkcraft movement. The Fujina kiln can be termed the parent kiln of these diverse kilns, having begun in approximately the middle of the eighteenth century as a tile kiln, then became a fief kiln in the nineteenth century, producing elegant wares alongside utility vessels. In the Meiji and Taishō periods it experienced cycles of prosperity and decline, then made a fresh start as a new folk kiln after 1925. The Funaki kiln became the center of activity and created Western tableware under Bernard Leach's inspiration, providing pots for contemporary living along with the Japanese tableware made until that time. The color tone of galena glaze and the method of using slip are unusual in Japan. A green glaze was frequently used on the old works, while bote-bote teabowls (note 16), teapots, and a local bowl type were specialties. Naturally, other utility vessels were also fired.

A contemporary folk kiln, the Shussai kiln, was created in Hikawa County in 1947. This kiln was established by young amateurs relying on Sōetsu Yanagi's aesthetic theory of crafts. Several items are being developed as contemporary folkcraft products.

Hand-warming braziers and kitchen grills made in in the technique of black roof tiles from Ōtsu, a small kiln in Izumo, are charming items.

Along the approximately sixty kilometers of seacoast of the Iwami district, from Ōta to Hamada, various kilns such as Ōta, Yunotsu, Gotsu, Kōfu, Hashi, and Hamada were established from the end of the eighteenth century through the nineteenth century, and, at the height of prosperity during the Meiji and Taishō periods, one hundred kilns were belching smoke. Employing Bizen technology, enormous kilns fired both large and small storage vats, storage jars, and large utility bowls, and today, also, huge climbing kilns reminiscent of that grandeur remain at various places. Moreover, this is also a production center for the lovely red roof tiles of the area, the production of which is still alive. The potters of these various seacoast kilns were famous for their skill with the potter's wheel and were often engaged to work here and there at other kilns. Great field storage jars, used as compost pits in fields, are found interred in the soil of the fields even today, and the large and small water storage jars used widely in western Japan, remind us of that skill. However, due to the pots' large size and the cost of labor and materials, almost all production has ceased.

The Kiami kilns, located to the west of Masuda, included a good folk kiln that fired small utility wares, but this, too, has perished. Moreover, Hagi ware, of Yamaguchi Prefecture in the west, is prominent as a tea ceramic, but the fact that there were good vessels among Hagi utility wares is made evident by the white-glazed pouring bowl from the Ōtsu kiln illustrated in Plate 20.

San'yō District (Okayama, Hiroshima, and Yamaguchi prefectures)

Folk kilns are comparatively less numerous in the San'yō district of Okayama, Hiroshima, and Yamaguchi prefectures than in San'in. This may be because Seto in the east and Karatsu in the west, both major ceramic centers, could be readily reached by boat through the Inland Sea.

Well-known Bizen ware is located in Okayama Prefecture. It is also called Imbe ware. Extolled from early on as a tea ceramic, the tea ceremony influence was reflected in its traditional utility vessels, but the great variety of such vessels preserved the integrity of the glazeless vitrified ware. This includes so-called boat saké bottles, with their broad, flat base, closely resembling those of Tamba, large storage jars, braziers, and mortars. The oil storage jar pictured in Plate 10 is one example of the small objects produced. Ōhara ware in Asakuchi County is a local kiln firing unglazed ware and black earthenware. Vessels such as cooking pots, teapots, pans for drying or baking foods, foot and bed warmers, charcoal extinguishing jars (live coals were placed in these ceramic jars after use to be safely extinguished), and kitchen grills were fired black using roof-tile making techniques; octopus and goby pots were unglazed. These are primitive and artless pots, attractive for that reason.

Kurashiki has the Sakatsu and Hajima kilns. Sakatsu began as a folk kiln in 1876, but sometime after 1925 it became the kiln of an artist-potter, under the influence of Hamada, Kawai, and Leach. However, it can still be regarded as a contemporary folk kiln concentrating on utility vessels. Starting after World War II, Kurashiki-Minato and Sakatsu-Tsutsumi kilns are refreshing contemporary kilns tackling the mass-production of tableware. Hajima is a folk kiln that opened in 1946, separating itself from Sakatsu. It likewise makes sundry tableware.

Niimi ware, which appeared around 1897, is situated in Niimi City. A descendant in the Iwami line, it supplied neighboring farm households with kitchen utensils such as persimmon (note 27) and black-glazed storage jars. At one time it was waning, but recently signs of regeneration have been visible.

At Happonmatsu in Hiroshima Prefecture, an unglazed earthenware kiln flourished from the end of the Edo period through the Meiji period. It was a humble folk ware called Hara no Handō, produced as a sideline by farming households and distributed throughout the prefecture. A little is still being fired today.

In Yamaguchi Prefecture, Horikoshi ware can be found on the outskirts of Bōfu. It is said to have been established in approximately the middle of the eighteenth century. It was the most prosperous large folk kiln not only in Yamaguchi Prefecture but in San'yō. In the early Shōwa period, some ten kilns were firing such wares as saké bottles, large lidded storage jars, water storage jars, mortars, field storage jars (note 26) and marketing them as far as central Honshu and Shikoku. Although now planters have become the principal products, the storage jars made from time to time have still not lost their power. Near there, the Sano kiln, which fired earthenware pots of rustic charm for *dobin mushi* (a broth simmered in a small teapot), no longer exists.

1. Government kilns (*kan'yō*). Official government kilns that made utensils for the imperial court of China. Imperial kiln wares were extravagant and finely crafted. Kilns under the supervision of the Japanese imperial court were also established in Japan in the Nara period (645–794), but died out during the middle ages.

2. Fief kilns (*han'yō*). Kilns under the patronage and protection of Edo period (1615–1868) fiefs, established primarily to bolster a fief's economy. Despite being fief kilns, many of them fired folk wares, and not a few became folk kilns.

3. Muneyoshi (Sōetsu) Yanagi (1889–1961). Philosopher and aesthetician. From his youthful days as a member of the group associated with the *Shirakaba* ("White Birch") literary magazine, he was active in the spheres of religion, philosophy, and art. He coined the phrase *mingei* and led the folkcraft movement. He founded the Japan Folkcraft Musum in 1936, becoming its first curator. Researching and presenting the arts and crafts of the common people of Japan as well as other countries, preserving and developing handwork, establishing a theory of the beauty of arts and crafts, he initiated diverse endeavors and, in his later years, devoted himself to the study of Buddhist aesthetics.

4. Courtyard ceramics (*oniwa-yaki*). A kiln or the products of such a kiln, producing tea wares or other elegant wares in the taste of the lord of a fief. Many such kilns began by making courtyard ceramics then developed into official fief kilns or into folk kilns.

5. Black glaze (*kuro gusuri*). A dark glaze of the purple family, containing cobalt or manganese oxide. Common on utility wares during and after the Meiji period (1868–1912). Cf. *tenmoku* glaze, note 17.

6. *Nuka* white (*nuka-jiro*; rice bran or rice-bran-ash white). A white glaze based on rice bran ash. Often used as a drip glaze.

7. *Ame* ("amber") glaze. One of the iron glazes. Oxidation produces a warm amber; reduction, a dark color.

8. *Namako* (literally, "sea cucumber") glaze. One of the unvitrified glazes. The glaze color is not uniform and has fine speckles or streaks of white, purple, and indigo. It is used frequently in the Tōhoku region and in other widely scattered folk kilns.

9. Shōji Hamada (1894–1978). Potter of worldwide renown. In 1920 he accompanied Bernard Leach to England and worked with Leach in St. Ives, Cornwall, during the first year of The Leach Pottery. In 1924, upon his return to Japan, settled down in Tochigi Prefecture at Mashiko and made ceramics. Along with Muneyoshi Yanagi and Kanjirō Kawai, he was active as a leader of the folkcraft movement. After Yanagi's death, he assumed the posts of curator of the Japan Folkcraft Museum and of chairman of the Japan Folkcraft Society.

10. Helmet bowl (*kabuto bachi*) A wide, deep bowl closely resembling a helmet.

11. Rifle kiln (*teppō gama*). A type of early climbing kiln with either a single, long chamber or a few long chambers. In Tachikui this type of kiln is still being used today.

12. *Suna-e gosu* (literally, "sand picture cobalt"). A natural cobalt (containing manganese and iron impurities) from Mino and Seto. Used both as an ingredient for producing blue overglaze enamel decoration and for underglaze cobalt decoration (*sometsuke*). Differing in hue from the *gosu* mined in China (*kara gosu*), the quality of the color is softer and closer to a dark violet. Although *suna-e gosu* is also called "mountain" *gosu* (*yama gosu*), in Kyushu the latter term refers instead to the high iron content *gosu* mined in China, which turns a dark greenish-brown in oxidation firing.

13. *Oni-ita*. A name used in Seto for a type of limonite (brown iron oxide ore). Besides being utilized in *tenmoku* glaze, it is frequently used for underglaze iron decoration.

14. Rouge pot (*beni bachi*). A) A tea ceremony charcoal brazier on which the tea kettle is heated. B) A Seto utility bowl or dish-shaped vessel with a thick inverted rim and wide, shallow bowl.

15. Shudei ware (*shudei-yaki*). Reddish-brown, unglazed, vitrified ceramics produced at the Yi-hsing kiln in Kiangsu Province, China. A similar ware is found in Japan, consisting primarily of small teapots and tea cups. Similar to Banko ware.

16. *Bote-bote* teabowl (*bote-bote chawan*). These bowls are primarily used in the Izumo region (Shimane Prefecture) to hold tea-and-rice gruel (*cha gayu*). The same type of bowl is called a "Gorohachi" or "Goroshichi" teabowl throughout northern Kyushu, Shikoku, and the Chūgoku region. While the *bote-bote* bowl is usually glazed green, the term "*gosu* (cobalt) style teabowl" is also used.

17. *Tenmoku* glaze. A saturated iron glaze that fires black or brown. Although it is said to have been the glaze on the everyday vessels of a Ch'an Buddhist temple on T'ien-mu (Japanese, Tenmoku) Mountain in Chekiang Province in China, it was a common glaze used on utility vessels. It was used on Seto teabowls during the Kamakura period (1185–1333). Kiln effects (*yōhen*) were frequently produced during firing, and special terms for them have been coined.

18. Kawai kiln. Kanjirō Kawai located his kiln in the Gojōzaka district of Kyoto. This term also designates works by potters under the tutelage of Kanjirō Kawai (1890–1966).

19. Seven Enshū Kilns. The seven kilns where Kobori Enshū (note 20) had tea wares fired to his order: Shidoro in Shizuoka Prefecture; Asahi in Uji; old Sobe (*ko Sobe*) in Hyōgo Prefecture; Akahada in Nara Prefecture; Agano and Takatori, both in Fukuoka Prefecture.

20. Kobori Enshū (1579–1647). A major tea master of the early Edo period. After serving the Toyotomi clan, he entered the service of the first three Tokugawa shoguns, holding the Enshū fief and the posts of Minister of Works and Administrator of Fushimi Township. He studied the tea ceremony under Furuta Oribe (1544–1615). He was skilled at architecture, landscaping of gardens, flower arrangement, and tea utensil design.

21. "Ink flow" (*sumi nagashi*). Marbelized effect made with dark and white slip.

22. *Haikaburi*. The natural or accidental ash glaze resulting from large amounts of ash from the firewood (usually pine) being deposited on vessels during the firing process and fusing to form a glaze. This effect is frequently seen on old Tamba, Shigaraki, and Bizen wares.

23. Shōya Yoshida (1898–1972). A doctor who was in sympathy with Muneyoshi Yanagi's folkcraft movement. While practicing medicine, he directed the San'in New Folkcraft Movement and instituted the Tottori Folkcraft Museum, becoming curator. In addition, he laid plans for the Tottori Folkcraft Cooperative, the Takumi Folkcraft Shop, and Takumi cuisine, and established the manufacture, marketing, and use of new folkcrafts on a practical basis.

24. Galena glaze. A lead glaze often used on earthenware. Though it is common in Europe, Fujina developed this glaze independently. From the Meiji period (1868–1912) onward, it was used at a number of kilns.

25. Bernard Leach (1857–1979). English ceramic artist. Setting out on his artistic career as an etcher, he was attracted to Japan and arrived there in 1909. He formed a friendship with the members of the *Shirakaba* ("White Birch"; a literary magazine) group, especially Muneyoshi Yanagi. He soon developed an interest in ceramics and studied *raku* ware under the sixth generation Ōgata Kenzan. He associated closely with Kenkichi Tomimoto, Shōji Hamada and Kanjirō Kawai, later joining forces with the folkcraft movement as well. In 1920 he established a kiln at St. Ives, Cornwall, developing a style that sought a harmony of the Orient and the Occident.

26. Field storage jar (*no tsubo*). A large storage jar that is used as a compost pit in farm fields.

27. Persimmon glaze (*kaki gusuri*). A brown or red-brown iron glaze, produced by oxidation firing. Often found on folk ceramics.

Folk Kilns of Honshu

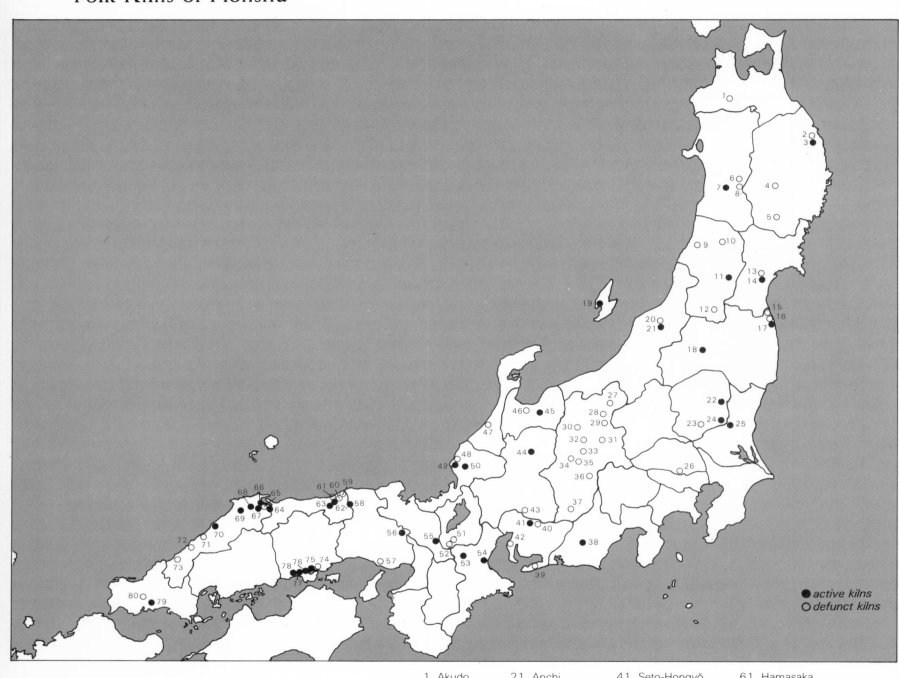

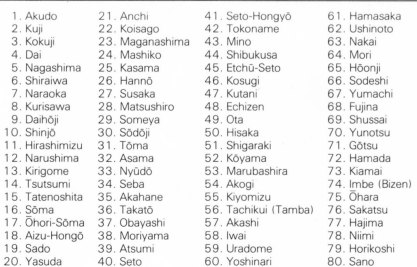

1. Akudo	21. Anchi	41. Seto-Hongyō	61. Hamasaka
2. Kuji	22. Koisago	42. Tokoname	62. Ushinoto
3. Kokuji	23. Maganashima	43. Mino	63. Nakai
4. Dai	24. Mashiko	44. Shibukusa	64. Mori
5. Nagashima	25. Kasama	45. Etchū-Seto	65. Hōonji
6. Shiraiwa	26. Hannō	46. Kosugi	66. Sodeshi
7. Naraoka	27. Susaka	47. Kutani	67. Yumachi
8. Kurisawa	28. Matsushiro	48. Echizen	68. Fujina
9. Daihōji	29. Someya	49. Ota	69. Shussai
10. Shinjō	30. Sōdōji	50. Hisaka	70. Yunotsu
11. Hirashimizu	31. Tōma	51. Shigaraki	71. Gōtsu
12. Narushima	32. Asama	52. Kōyama	72. Hamada
13. Kirigome	33. Nyūdō	53. Marubashira	73. Kiamai
14. Tsutsumi	34. Seba	54. Akogi	74. Imbe (Bizen)
15. Tatenoshita	35. Akahane	55. Kiyomizu	75. Ōhara
16. Sōma	36. Takatō	56. Tachikui (Tamba)	76. Sakatsu
17. Ōhori-Sōma	37. Obayashi	57. Akashi	77. Hajima
18. Aizu-Hongō	38. Moriyama	58. Iwai	78. Niimi
19. Sado	39. Atsumi	59. Uradome	79. Horikoshi
20. Yasuda	40. Seto	60. Yoshinari	80. Sano

1

2

3

4

5

6

1. *Kutani ware. Plate, heron and reeds design, overglaze enamels. D. 19.8 cm. Middle Edo period.*

2. *Kutani ware. Small jar, circular medallions, overglaze enamels. H. 10.9 cm. Middle Edo period. Japan Folkcraft Museum.*

3. *Banko ware. Two incense stands, lotus blossom designs, overglaze enamels. Left: H. 6.3 cm. Late Edo period. Japan Folkcraft Museum.*

4. *Kutani ware. Saké cup, sea bream design, overglaze enamels. D. at the mouth 8.6 cm. Late Edo period. Japan Folkcraft Museum.*

5. *Yoshinari ware. Lidded jar, scattered plum design, underglaze cobalt. H. 16.4 cm. Meiji period. Tottori Folkcraft Museum.*

6. *Shibukusa ware. Incense stand, deer design, underglaze cobalt. D. at the mouth 13.3 cm. Meiji period. Kusakabe Folkcraft Museum.*

17

7

8

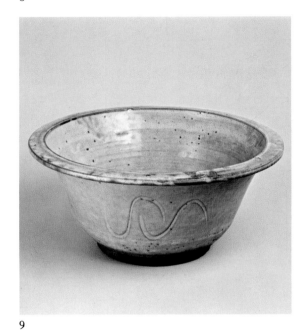

9

10

11

SAN'YŌ REGION (7–15)

7. *Horikoshi ware. Large wide-mouthed storage jar, paddled texturing, dripped white and splashed cobalt glazes on a black ground. H. 54.3 cm. Modern. Kurashiki Folkcraft Museum.*

8. *Sakatsu ware. Lidded pot, amber glaze on a white ground. H. 15.8 cm. Modern. Kurashiki Folkcraft Museum.*

9. *Sakatsu ware. Deep bowl, incised line design, white glaze. D. at the mouth 35.8 cm. Modern. Kurashiki Folkcraft Museum.*

10. *Bizen ware. Square oil bottle with impressed decoration, unglazed. H. 20.8 cm. Meiji period. Kurashiki Folkcraft Museum.*

11. *Mushiake ware. Large saké bottle, overlapping brown and transparent glazes, iron oxide chrysanthemum design. H. 30.2 cm. Meiji period. Kurashiki Folkcraft Museum.*

12

13

14

15

12. *Hajima ware. Pedestaled dish, green glaze. D. 22.7 cm. Modern. Kurashiki Folkcraft Museum.*

13. *Hajima ware. Bowl, namako glaze inside and trailed design on a brown ground. D. 18.3 cm. Modern. Kurashiki Folkcraft Museum.*

14. *Niimi ware. Large lidded storage jar, black drip glaze on a brown glaze ground. H. 55.3 cm. Kurashiki Folkcraft Museum.*

15. *Sakatsu ware, Minato kiln. Large bowl, overlapping light and dark drip glazes. D. 40.2 cm. Modern. Kurashiki Folkcraft Museum.*

16

17

18

19

20

21

SAN'IN REGION (16–28)

16. *Fujina ware. Kneading bowl, white glaze. D. 50.4 cm. Late Edo period. Izumo Folkcraft Museum.*

17. *Kiami ware. Lidded jar, black glaze. H. 13.8 cm. Modern. Izumo Folkcraft Museum.*

22

18. *Fujina ware. Large saké bottle, galena glaze. H. 22.4 cm. Meiji period.*

19. *Iwami ware. Mortar, iron glaze. D. 40.2 cm. Modern. Izumo Folkcraft Museum.*

20. *Ōtsu ware. Pouring bowl, white glaze. D. 21.8 cm. Meiji period. Kurashiki Folkcraft Museum.*

23

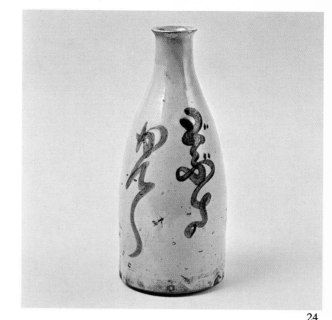

24

25

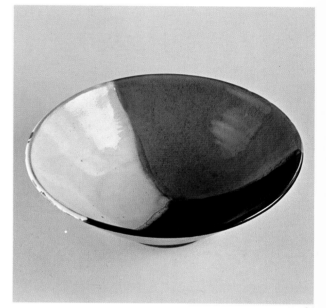

26

27

21. *Fujina ware. Large "eggplant" saké bottle, with partially overlapping black and white glazes. H. 34.2 cm. Meiji period. Izumo Folkcraft Museum.*

22. *Fujina ware. Three bowl types, green glazes. Right: D. 20.1 cm. Izumo Folkcraft Museum.*

23. *Iwami ware. Four saké bottles, iron oxide, cobalt and slip decoration, transparent glaze. Left: H. 25.7 cm. 1920s to present. Izumo Folkcraft Museum.*

24. *Ushinoto ware. Saké bottle, iron oxide characters, transparent glaze. H. 21.3 cm. Meiji period. Tottori Folkcraft Museum.*

28

25. *Ushinoto ware. Large jar with three-color thrown glaze on a brown ground. H. 50.4 cm. Meiji period. Kurashiki Folkcraft Museum.*

26. *Ushinoto ware. Bowl with black, green, and white glazes. D. 30.5 cm. Modern. Kurashiki Folkcraft Museum.*

27. *Ōtsu ware. Roof-tile ware hand-warmer. H. 23.6 cm. Modern. Izumo Folkcraft Museum.*

28. *Ushinoto ware. "Gorohachi" bowl, blue-green glaze. D. 10.2 cm. Meiji period. Tottori Folkcraft Museum.*

29

31

32

33

30

34

35

36

TAMBA WARE (29–36)

29. Tachikui ware. "Boat" saké bottle, natural ash glaze, akadobe red slip ground. H. 27.9 cm. Middle Edo period. Japan Folkcraft Museum.

30. Tachikui ware. Small storage jar, incised fish design, black glaze. H. 21.1 cm. Middle Edo period. Japan Folkcraft Museum.

31. Tachikui ware. Saké bottle, amber glaze on a white ground. H. 15.5 cm. Late Edo period. Japan Folkcraft Museum.

32. Tachikui ware. Saké bottle, tube-trailed line pattern. H. 20.9 cm. Late Edo period. Japan Folkcraft Museum.

33. Tachikui ware. Saké bottle, tube-trailed logo. H. 16.6 cm. Late Edo period. Japan Folkcraft Museum.

34. Tachikui ware. "Boat" saké bottle, leaf resist, black glaze drip on akadobe red slip ground. H. 32.5 cm. Middle Edo period. Japan Folkcraft Museum.

35. Tachikui ware. Small jar, white slip drip effect, transparent glaze. H. 12.1 cm. Late Edo period. Japan Folkcraft Museum.

36. Tachikui ware. Small jar, "ink flow" slip effect, transparent glaze. H. 11.2 cm. Late Edo period. Japan Folkcraft Museum.

37

38

39

40

41

42

ECHIZEN AND ETCHŪ REGIONS (37–42)

37. Hisaka ware. Large lidded jar, rice-bran-ash white glaze on an amber glaze ground. H. 41.3 cm. Modern. Japan Folkcraft Museum.

38. Etchū–Seto ware. Wide-mouthed jar with rice-bran-ash white glaze on an amber glaze ground. H. 21.4 cm. Meiji period. Toyama Municipal Folkcraft Museum.

39. Ota ware. Large wide-mouthed jar, unglazed, modeled cord decoration. D. at the mouth 48.4 cm. Late Edo period. Toyama Municipal Folkcraft Museum.

40. Ota ware. Large jar, ash drip glaze. H. 59.6 cm. Late Edo period. Toyama Municipal Folkcraft Museum.

41. Kosugi ware. Oil lamp with green glaze. H. 13.2 cm. Late Edo period. Toyama Municipal Folkcraft Museum.

42. Kosugi ware. Right: bowl with trailed green glaze. D. 10.2 cm. Left: bowl with trailed black glaze. D. 9.8 cm. Both Meiji period. Toyama Municipal Folkcraft Museum.

43

44

45

46

SETO AND MINO WARES (43–52)

43. Mino ware. "Gong" bowl, Oribe green glaze and iron oxide designs. D. 34.7 cm. Middle Edo period. Japan Folkcraft Museum.

44. Seto ware. Household latar vase, amber glaze. H. 17.7 cm. Late Edo period.

45. Mino ware. Five water droppers (suiteki). Upper right: design of bamboo and the character for "tiger." L. 8.9 cm. Middle to late Edo period. Japan Folkcraft Museum.

46. Mino ware. Grater, white glaze. H. 5.9 cml Late Edo period. Japan Folkcraft Museum.

47

48

49

50

51

52

47. *Seto ware. Bowl, iron oxide pine needle pattern and cobalt splotches. D. 11.6 cm. Late Edo period. Japan Folkcraft Museum.*

48. *Seto ware. Bowl, iron oxide net design. D. 11.6 cm. Late Edo period.*

49. *Seto ware. Saké bottle, iron oxide scroll pattern. H. 31.3 cm. Late Edo period. Japan Folkcraft Museum.*

50. *Seto ware. Right: rice bowl. D. 12.2 cm. Left: pouring bowl. H. 7.9 cm. "Wheat straw" pattern. Japan Folkcraft Museum.*

51. *Seto ware. Small plate, cobalt floral design. D. 13.2 cm. Middle Edo period. Japan Folkcraft Museum.*

52. *Seto ware. Incense stand, cobalt lotus flower design. H. 7.8 cm. Japan Folkcraft Museum.*

53

54

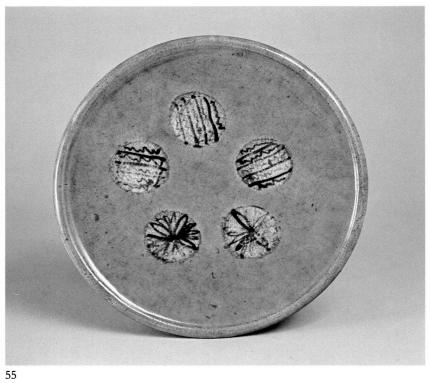

55

56

57

58

59

"PICTURE" PLATES (53–59)

53. Seto ware. Oil plate (abura-zara), dipped in Oribe green glaze, iron oxide design of nets drying. D. 23.0 cm. Late Edo period. Japan Folkcraft Museum.

54. Seto ware. Oil plate (abura-zara), dipped in Oribe green glaze, iron oxide landscape design. D. 21.9 cm. Late Edo period.

55. Seto ware. Oil plate (abura-zara), medallions with cobalt patterns on a green ground. D. 22.3 cm. Late Edo period. Japan Folkcraft Museum.

56. Seto ware. Oil plate (abura-zara), iron oxide design of clouds and crane. D. 22.0 cm. Late Edo period.

57. Seto ware. Plate, iron oxide "horse-eye" pattern. D. 35.6 cm. Late Edo period. Japan Folkcraft Museum.

58. Seto ware. Stone plate (ishi-zara), iron oxide and cobalt willow design. D. 26.5 cm. Late Edo period. Japan Folkcraft Museum.

59. Seto ware. Stone plate (ishi-zara), iron oxide and cobalt landscape design. D. 36.0 cm. Late Edo period. Japan Folkcraft Museum.

60

61

62

TEAPOTS (60–69)

60. Marubashira ware. Teapot, green glaze. H. 18.2 cm. Meiji period. Japan Folkcraft Museum.

61. Fujina ware. Teapot, green glaze. H. 13.2 cm. Meiji period.

62. Akashi ware. Teapot, brushmark and iron decoration. H. 22.8 cm. 1912–25. Japan Folkcraft Museum.

63. Shussai ware. Bancha (tea for everyday use) vessels, black circular motifts on a brown ground. Teapot: H. 15.3 cm.; Tea cups: H. 5.7 cm. Modern.

64. Mashiko ware. Teapot, "window picture" design of plum blossoms. H 8.9 cm. 1912–25. Japan Folkcraft Museum.

65. Sōma ware. Teapot, blue-green glaze. H. 12.1 cm. Late Edo period. Matsumoto Folkcraft Museum.

66. Kōyama ware. Teapot, landscape drawing. H. 9.4 cm. 1912–25. Japan Folkcraft Museum.

67. Nyūdō ware. Handled teapot, white drip glaze on a black ground. H. 27.9 cm. Meiji period. Matsumoto Folk Art and Life Museum.

68. Mashiko ware. Teapot with landscape design. H. 17.2 cm. Modern.

69. Ōhara ware. Roof-tile ware teapot. H. 19.4 cm. Modern. Kurashiki Folkcraft Museum.

63

64

65

66

67

68

69

70

71

72

SHINSHŪ REGION (70–80)

70. *Seba ware. Large pouring bowl,* namako *glaze on a brown ground. H. 18.5 cm. Late Edo period. Matsumoto Folk Art and Life Museum.*

71. *Takatō ware. Steamer, white glaze. H. 26.8 cm. Meiji period. Matsumoto Folk Art and Life Museum.*

72. *Matsushiro ware. Tub, white drip glaze on a "buckwheat" glaze ground. H. 19.5 cm. Meiji period. Matsumoto Folkcraft Museum.*

73

74

75

76. *Matsushiro ware. Large saké bottle, green drip glaze. H. 40.8 cm. Late Edo period. Matsumoto Folk Art and Life Museum.*

73. *Matsushiro ware. Bowl (soba-gaki wan) for mixing dumplings made of buckwheat (soba) flour and hot water, white drip glaze on a "buckwheat" glaze. H. 8.2 cm. Late Edo period. Matsumoto Folkcraft Museum.*

74. *Takatō ware. "Fire container," partially overlapping amber and white glazes. H. 11.1 cm. Meiji period. Matsumoto Folkcraft Museum.*

75. *Matsushiro ware. Small storage jar, white drip glaze on a "buckwheat" glaze. H. 20.2 cm. Meiji period.*

77

78

79

80

32

77. *Seba ware. Lidded storage jar, white drip glaze on a brown ground. H. 43.5 cm. Meiji period. Matsumoto Folkcraft Museum.*

78. *Someya ware. Storage jar, natural ash glaze and "drawstring" mouth. H. 32.8 cm. Late Edo period. Matsumoto Folkcraft Museum.*

79. *Takatō ware. Strainer, white glaze. H. 26.4 cm. Meiji period. Matsumoto Folkcraft Museum.*

80. *Matsushiro ware. Large saké bottle, green drip glaze on a white ground. H. 36.9 cm. Meiji period. Matsumoto Folkcraft Museum.*

81

83

82

KANTŌ REGION (81–83)

81. *Kasama ware. Lidded jar, two-colored drip glaze on a white ground. H. 28.7 cm. Modern. Japan Folkcraft Museum.*

82. *Maganoshima ware. Earthenware brush stands. Black: H. 13.3 cm. Red: H. 13.8 cm. Modern. Japan Folkcraft Museum.*

83. *Mashiko ware. Medium-sized plate, flower designs in wax-resist circles on a black ground. D. 13.1 cm. Modern. Japan Folkcraft Museum.*

84

85

86

TŌHOKU REGION (84–94)

84. Aizu-Hongō ware, Munakata kiln. Lidded jar, green drip glaze on a white ground. H. 21.9 cm. Japan Folkcraft Museum.

85. Aizu-Hongō ware, Munakata kiln. Large bowl, namako glaze on an amber glaze ground. D. 47.3 cm. Japan Folkcraft Museum.

86. Aizu-Hongō ware, Munakata kiln. Herring dish with namako glaze on an amber glaze ground. H. 12.1 cm. Japan Folkcraft Museum.

87. Tatenoshita ware. Large jar, rice-bran-ash glaze on a black glaze ground. H. 62.1 cm. Late Edo period. Japan Folkcraft Museum.

88. Aizu-Hongō ware, Munakata kiln. Storage jar, white and green glazes on a white ground. H. 48.3 cm. Japan Folkcraft Museum.

87

88

89

90

89. *Hirashimizu ware. Pouring bowl, white glaze. H. 12.8 cm. Modern. Japan Folkcraft Museum.*

90. *Kuji Ware. Pouring bowl, white glaze on a black ground. H. 12.6 cm. Two cups for sauce in which soba (buckwheat noodles) are dipped, green glaze and amber glaze. Modern. Japan Folkcraft Museum.*

91. *Left: Shinjō ware. Cooking pot, namako glaze. D. at mouth 24.5 cm. Modern. Japan Folkcraft Museum.*
Middle: Daihōji ware. Steamer, white glaze. D. at mouth 17.7 cm. Modern. Japan Folkcraft Museum.
Right: Kurisawa ware. Pouring bowl, namako glaze. D. at mouth 22.5 cm. Modern. Japan Folkcraft Museum.

92. *Left: Naraoka ware. Lidded jar, namako glaze. H. 28.3 cm. Modern. Japan Folkcraft Museum.*
Right: Shiraiwa ware. Vase for household altar, namako glaze. H. 12.6 cm. Modern. Japan Folkcraft Museum.

93. *Nagashima ware. Storage jar, white glaze on a brown ground. H. 36.4 cm. Japan Folkcraft Museum.*

91

92

93

94

94. *Tsutsumi ware. Three-to capacity (14.4 U.S. gallons or 54 liters) water storage jar, rice-bran-ash glaze on a black glaze ground. D. at mouth 35.8 cm.; H. 39.6 cm. Late Edo period. Japan Folkcraft Museum.*

Plate Notes

1. *Kutani ware. Plate, heron and reeds design, overglaze enamels. D. 19.8 cm. Middle Edo period.*
A superb work displaying "awkward" charm. The serene brush style is refreshing. It may be one of a set.

2. *Kutani ware. Small jar, circular medallions, overglaze enamels. H. 10.9 cm. Middle Edo period. Japan Folkcraft Museum.*
A fine work. The circular medallion decoration is succinct and exuberant, enhanced by the deep enamel colors. It may be a medicine jar. The lively design and fluency of the brushwork are evidence that such pieces were made in quantity.

3. *Banko wares. Two incense stands, lotus blossom designs, overglaze enamels. Left: H. 6.3 cm. Late Edo period. Japan Folkcraft Museum.*
Such stands for incense sticks were used on household Buddhist altars.

4. *Kutani ware. Saké cup, sea bream design, overglaze enamels. D. at the mouth 8.6 cm. Late Edo period. Japan Folkcraft Museum.*
A saké cup for use on auspicious occasions; a mass-produced item from the Kutani folk kilns.

5. *Yoshinari ware. Lidded jar, scattered plum design, underglaze cobalt. H. 16.4 cm. Meiji period. Tottori Folkcraft Museum.*
The Imari style of underglaze cobalt decoration was emulated at porcelain kilns throughout the country.

7. *Horikoshi ware. Large, wide-mouthed storage jar, paddled texturing, dripped white and splashed cobalt glazes on a black ground. H. 54.3 cm. Modern. Kurashiki Folkcraft Museum.*
Horikoshi in Yamaguchi Prefecture is another kiln whose traditional work has recently been revived. This large storage jar was used in the fields for fertilizer or for water. There is personality in the paddled texturing and in the glaze application, in which a small amount of cobalt was splashed on the running white glaze.

9. *Sakatsu ware. Deep bowl, inscribed line design, white glaze. D. at the mouth 35.8 cm. Modern. Kurashiki Folkcraft Museum.*
Since the kiln opened at the beginning of the Meiji period, Sakatsu ware, by virtue of the labor of its adept potters, supplied utility wares to the area encompassing Hiroshima, Okayama, and Yamaguchi prefectures. After 1925, with the guidance of the folkcraft movement, it assimilated various techniques. Plates 8 and 9 are the result of this assimilation, and the pieces may be called new folk ceramics. The distinguishing features of Hajima and Sakatsu wares are their lightness and calmness, typical of the Seto Inland Sea area.

11. *Mushiake ware. Large saké bottle, overlapping brown and transparent glazes, iron oxide chrysanthemum design. H. 30.2 cm. Meiji period. Kurashiki Folkcraft Museum.*
Mushiake was a fief kiln in Mushiake, Oku County, Okayama Prefecture, which, beginning in the Bunkyū era (1861–64), became a folk kiln and prospered until the early years of the Meiji period. The glazed utility wares of Mushiake competed with the nearby unglazed Bizen (Imbe) wares. Various saké bottles decorated with the "four princely plants" (plum, orchid, bamboo, and chrysanthemum) were a specialty. The bottle illustrated here is one example, and the overlapping of the glazes is superb.

13. *Hajima ware. Bowl, namako glaze inside and trailed design on a brown ground. D. at the mouth 18.3 cm. Modern. Kurashiki Folkcraft Museum.*
Hajima ware began in 1946. Based on the techniques of Sakatsu ware and gradually expressing its own unique characteristics, it has continued to the present. Plate 13 illustrates a bowl that comes in a variety of sizes, and, unusual in the San'yō region, uses the *namako* glaze. The trailed pattern of wavy and straight lines is fresh.

14. *Niimi ware. Large lidded storage jar, black drip glaze on a brown glaze ground. H. 55.3 cm. Kurashiki Folkcraft Museum.*
It is heartening to see this once-declining kiln recovering. Given the proper conditions, folk kilns have the capacity to revive. With the technology of the Iwami ware heritage, Niimi's future is optimistic.

15. *Sakatsu ware, Minato kiln. Large bowl, overlapping light and dark drip glazes. D. at the mouth 40.2 cm. Modern. Kurashiki Folkcraft Museum.*
The Minato kiln, together with the Tsutsumi kiln, rose in Sakatsu after World War II, and having assimilated techniques from many places, is actively mass-producing everyday tableware. This bowl has an intimacy in the texture of the clay and the novel design of the drip glaze flowing toward the center.

16. *Fujina ware. Kneading bowl, white glaze. D. at the mouth 50.4 cm. Late Edo period. Izumo Folkcraft Museum (entrusted).*
The full shape can probably be attributed to its use for kneading *soba* (buckwheat noodle) dough.

19. *Iwami ware. Mortar, iron glaze. D. at the mouth 40.2 cm. Modern. Izumo Folkcraft Museum (entrusted).*
The typical Iwami ware brown glaze contains *kimachi*, a locally mined sandstone.

20. *Ōtsu ware. Pouring bowl, white glaze. D. at the mouth 21.8 cm. Meiji period. Kurashiki Folkcraft Museum.*
A vessel from a folk kiln associated with Hagi ware.

22. *Fujina ware. Three bowl types, green glazes. Right: D. at the mouth 20.1 cm. Izumo Folkcraft Museum (entrusted).*
The middle-sized and the small one are *bote-bote* teabowls (note 16). The large one is probably a vessel for side dishes. Symbolic of the simple, warm, and serene Izumo area.

23. *Iwami ware. Four saké bottles, iron oxide, cobalt and slip decoration, transparent glaze. Left: H. 25.7 cm. 1920s to present. Izumo Folkcraft Museum (entrusted).*
These saké bottles indicate that Ushinoto in Shimane Prefecture and Iwami are closely related. The location of the kiln where Iwami saké bottles were made is unknown.

27. *Ōtsu ware. Roof-tile ware hand-warmer. H. 23.6 cm. Modern. Izumo Folkcraft Museum (entrusted).*
A hanging "temple bell" shaped hand-warming brazier for use on a fishing boat.

28. *Ushinoto ware. "Gorohachi" bowl, blue-green glaze. D. at the mouth 10.2 cm. Meiji period. Tottori Folkcraft Museum.*
Such bowls were used for water, tea, or saké.

29. *Tachikui ware. "Boat" saké bottle, natural ash glaze, aka-dobe red slip ground. H. 27.9 cm. Middle Edo period. Japan Folkcraft Museum.*
"Boat" saké bottles have wide bottoms to make them as stable as possible for use on boats and ships.

30. *Tachikui ware. Small storage jar, incised fish design, black glaze. H. 21.1 cm. Middle Edo period. Japan Folkcraft Museum.*
A utility vessel rather than a tea ceremony water container.

31. *Tachikui ware. Saké bottle, amber glaze on a white ground. H. 15.5 cm. Late Edo period. Japan Folkcraft Museum.*
This form is known as a "candle saké bottle" (*rōsoku tokkuri*) because of its resemblance to the shape of the traditional Japanese candle.

34. *Tachikui ware. "Boat" saké bottle, leaf resist, black glaze drip on* akadobe *red slip ground. H. 32.5 cm. Middle Edo period. Japan Folkcraft Museum.*
Plates 29 and 34 are masterpieces of Tamba folk wares, admired for their charm and the fact that one never tires of them.

35. *Tachikui ware. Small jar, white slip drip effect, transparent glaze. H. 12.1 cm. Late Edo period. Japan Folkcraft Museum.*
These small jars for pickled fish intestines *(uruka)* or pickled *sansho* peppercorns. "Ink flow" and slip drip effects are specialties of Tamba.

37. *Hisaka ware. Large lidded jar, rice-bran-ash white glaze on an amber glaze ground. H. 41.3 cm. Modern. Japan Folkcraft Museum.*
A major work indicating the dignity of Hisaka ware before World War II. The form is calm and ample but orderly. The well-controlled runs of the meticulously trailed white glaze make a favorable impression. This holds seven *shō* (a *shō* is an old volume unit equivalent to 3.81 pints).

38. *Etchū-Seto ware. Wide-mouthed jar, rice-bran-ash white glaze on an amber glaze ground. H. 21.4 cm. Meiji period. Toyama Municipal Folkcraft Museum.*
A vessel used as a salt or *miso* (fermented bean paste) jar. As the kiln name indicates, the techniques fall in the Seto tradition.

39. *Ota ware. Large wide-mouthed jar, unglazed, modeled cord decoration. D. at the mouth 48.8 cm. Late Edo period. Toyama Municipal Folkcraft Museum.*
Drawing on the heritage of the old Echizen kilns, the Ota ware kilns produced large utility pots without interruption throughout the Edo period, and there are few examples among other local kilns of such solid, unglazed, vitrified wares. This is probably a farmhouse water storage jar.

40. *Ota ware. Large jar, ash drip glaze. H. 59.6 cm. Late Edo period. Toyama Municipal Folkcraft Museum.*
In this large jar with a lively drip glaze on its sturdy body, the spirit of old Echizen survives. It is probably a jar for grain storage.

41. *Kosugi ware. Oil lamp with green glaze. H. 13.2 cm. Late Edo period. Toyama Municipal Folkcraft Museum*
Kosugi ware was largely a sophisticated ware made for urban areas. A surprising originality of design is seen in its tea wares, saké wares, and utility vessels. This lamp was for an urban market. It is without artifice or ostentation.

42. *Kosugi ware. Right: Bowl with trailed green glaze. D. at the mouth 10.2 cm. Left: Bowl with trailed black glaze. D. at the mouth 9.8 cm. Both Meiji period. Toyama Municipal Folkcraft Museum.*
Bote-bote teabowls (note 16) were used for rice gruel made with tea, not water; these display interesting trailed glaze designs.

50. *Seto ware. Right: rice bowl. D. 12.2 cm. Left: pouring bowl. H. 7.9 cm. "Wheat straw" pattern. Japan Folkcraft Museum.*
The term "wheat straw" was bestowed by tea masters. Originally very cheap, everyday pots.

52. *Seto ware. Incense stand, cobalt lotus flower design. H. 7.8 cm. Japan Folkcraft Museum.*
Though a small piece, its form and design are of imposing stature.

54. *Seto ware. Oil plate (abura-zara), dipped in Oribe green glaze, iron oxide landscape design. D. 21.9 cm. Late Edo period.*
Oil plates are also known as *andon* plates (*andon-zara*). An *andon* is a paper-covered oil lamp.

60. *Marubashira ware. Teapot, green glaze. H. 18.2 cm. Meiji period. Japan Folkcraft Museum.*

The Marubashira kiln in Iga is also a production center for teapots. Blue-green glazes were popular, perhaps because the color is soothing.

62. *Akashi ware. Teapot, brushmark and iron decoration. H. 22.8 cm. 1912–25. Japan Folkcraft Museum.*

Before the Meiji period, Akashi and Shigaraki were ranked as two major kilns making teapots. This pot is especially large.

64. *Mashiko ware. Teapot, "window picture" design of plum blossoms. H. 8.9 cm. 1912–25. Japan Folkcraft Museum.*

Both the "window picture" and the landscape drawing are techniques found on Mashiko teapots.

65. *Sōma ware. Teapot, blue-green glaze. H. 12.1 cm. Late Edo period. Matsumoto Folkcraft Museum.*

This old-style teapot form, a variation of the boat shape, displays vivid blue-green glaze, "gun barrel" spout, and "mountain peak" lugs. The iron handle is a further indication of its antiquity.

66. *Kōyama ware. Teapot, landscape drawing. H. 9.4 cm. 1912–25. Japanese Folkcraft Museum.*

Kōyama is in Shigaraki, where "landscape" teapots originated.

67. *Nyūdō ware. Handled teapot, white drip glaze on a black ground. H. 27.9 cm. Meiji period. Matsumoto Folk Art and Life Museum.*

The rippled form of the ceramic handle reduces slippage.

69. *Ōhara ware. Roof-tile ware teapot. H. 19.4 cm. Modern. Kurashiki Folkcraft Museum.*

Satonoshō Town, Okayama Prefecture. For use on the old style of Japanese cookstove; the flange keeps the pot from falling into the fire.

70. *Seba ware. Large pouring bowl,* namako *glaze on a brown ground. H. 18.5 cm. Late Edo period. Matsumoto Folk Art and Life Museum.*

Endowed with an imposing size and dignity, this piece can be considered superior among the countless pouring bowls. In particular, the bluish-white drip glaze is applied with superb skill and has a grand strength, while the piece of broken pot adhering to the side only enhances the dignity of this vessel. Probably because it was considered a kiln "second," it has survived until this day; in the past such vessels were made in large numbers.

71. *Takatō ware. Steamer, white glaze. H. 26.8 cm. Meiji period. Matsumoto Folk Art and Life Museum.*

Among the many Takatō kilns, those such as the Marusen kiln, which sprang up in the Meiji period, produced many pots for use in the manufacture of silk thread. This steamer must also have been made so that threads could be pulled through it. What function was fulfilled by the vertical tube along one side or the two places where the rim is trimmed away is unclear.

72. *Matsushiro ware. Tub, white drip glaze on a "buckwheat" glaze ground. H. 19.5 cm. Meiji period. Matsumoto Folkcraft Museum.*

This shape emulates the form of a wooden tub. The bands that imitate the tub hoops provide a reliable grip, particularly if the contents are heavy. It may be a crock for Japanese pickles.

73. *Matsushiro ware. Bowl (soba-gaki wan) for mixing dumplings made of buckwheat (soba) flour and hot water, white drip glaze on a "buckwheat" glaze. H. 8.2 cm. Late Edo period. Matsumoto Folkcraft Museum.*

This domestic pot is appropriate to the Shinshū area (present-day Nagano Prefecture), which is famous for its buckwheat *(soba)*. It may also have been used as a soup or rice bowl. The way the white glaze mottles on the "buckwheat" ground is attractive. Tranquil and ordinary, it equals famous teabowls in quiet taste.

74. *Takatō ware. "Fire container," partially overlapping amber and white glazes. H. 11.1 cm. Meiji period. Matsumoto Folkcraft Museum.*

This "fire container" held a coal or two in a bed of ash and was placed on a smoker's tray along with an ashtray, etc., for lighting the traditional Japanese pipe (*kiseru*). This one is given character by the grooves in the body and use of contrasting glaze colors on top and bottom. The white glaze carries a natural bluish tinge similiar to the *namako* glaze (note 8).

75. *Matsushiro ware. Small storage jar, white drip glaze on "buckwheat" glaze. H. 20.2 cm. Meiji period.*

Like the mixing bowl for mixing buckwheat dumplings in Plate 73, a white glaze has been applied on a "buckwheat" glaze ground. Although the form makes one think that it might have been made as a tea ceremony container, it is a kitchen utensil for storing salt or *miso* (fermented bean paste). It may have had a lid.

76. *Matsushiro ware. Large saké bottle, green drip glaze. H. 40.8 cm. Late Edo period. Matsumoto Folk Art and Life Museum.*

A major work, rare even for Matsushiro ware, where most every kind of pot was made, it could have held saké, soy sauce, or oil. The glimpse of blue on the lower edge of the ample green glaze coating is sophisticated.

77. *Seba ware. Lidded storage jar, white drip glaze on a brown ground. H. 43.5 cm. Meiji period. Matsumoto Folkcraft Museum.*

A superb example of Seba ware, which drew on the techniques of Seto and Shigaraki wares. The accuracy of the crafting of the lid and the blue-green hues of the drip glaze are beautiful.

78. *Someya ware. Storage jar, natural ash glaze and "drawstring" mouth. H. 32.8 cm. Late Edo period. Matsumoto Folkcraft Museum.*

Someya ware is generally unglazed; the ancient technique of long firing until the clay is vitrified captures the solid, honest charm of Kamakura period (1185–1333) ceramics. The structure of its wide mouth is a special feature.

79. *Takatō ware. Strainer, white glaze. H. 26.4 cm. Meiji period. Matsumoto Folkcraft Museum.*
This strainer was used for the fermented bean paste (*miso*) that each household made for itself. The artless workmanship conveys a strong sense of intimacy.

80. *Matsushiro ware. Large saké bottle, green drip glaze on a white ground. H. 36.9 cm. Meiji period. Matsumoto Folkcraft Museum.*
The dark, thick green glaze seems to grasp the bottle from above. The effect is vivid.

81. *Kasama ware. Lidded jar, two-colored drip glaze on a white ground. H. 28.7 cm. Modern. Japan Folkcraft Museum.*
Compressed but not rigid. This vessel must have been ideally suited for pickling plums (*umeboshi*), etc. The brown and green drip glazes capture the ambience of the Kantō Plain.

82. *Maganoshima ware. Earthenware brush stands. Black: H. 13.3 cm. Red: H. 13.8 cm. Modern. Japan Folkcraft Museum.*
A new design making the most of roof-tile techniques. In both the black and red, the deep hues are handsome. These can also be used as chopstick holders or vases.

83. *Mashiko ware. Medium-sized plate, flower designs in wax-resist circles on a black ground. D. 13.1 cm. Modern. Japan Folkcraft Museum.*
Although Mashiko produced kitchen wares for about eighty years after ceramic activity started there in the 1850s, pieces remaining from that time are surprisingly scarce. Utility pots are broken with heavy use, obviously, but the fact that most have been lost can probably be attributed to earthquake and war damage also. This plate, with its "window pictures," is a postwar innovation, employing the wax resist technique. The teapots that made Mashiko ware famous are shown in Plates 64 and 68.

87. *Tatenoshita ware. Large jar with rice-bran-ash glaze on a black glaze ground. H. 62.1 cm. Late Edo period. Japan Folkcraft Museum.*
A superb piece with strength and seasoned dignity.

88. *Aizu-Hongō ware, Munakata kiln. Storage jar, white and green glazes on a white ground. H. 48.3 cm. Japan Folkcraft Museum.*
The sturdy storage jar in Plate 88 is modestly decorated. The lidded vessel (Plate 84) is used for food, and the "herring dish" (Plate 86) is used for pickled herring. The large bowl is a postwar innovation. The Munakata kiln is vigorous today, upholding the folk kiln tradition of the Tōhoku region. These are all modern pieces.

94. *Tsutsumi ware. Three-to capacity water storage jar, rice-bran-ash glaze on a black glaze ground. D. at mouth 35.8 cm.; H. 39.6 cm. Late Edo period. Japan Folkcraft Museum.*
Large water storage jars of 3 *to*, 4 *to*, and 5 *to* (an old volume unit; one *to* is 4.8 U.S. gallons or 18 liters) sizes are the pride of Tsutsumi ware. The form as well as the glaze application of this storage jar leave nothing to be desired. It is a superb work exemplifying not only Tsutsumi ware but all Tōhoku region folk kilns.

定価2,900円
in Japan